the NLT
BIBLE
PROMISE
BOOK
for men

Tyndale House Publishers, Inc., Carol Stream, Illinois

Visit Tyndale online at www.tyndale.com and www.newlivingtranslation.com.

TYNDALE, New Living Translation, NLT, the New Living Translation logo, and Tyndale's quill logo are registered trademarks of Tyndale House Publishers, Inc.

The NLT Bible Promise Book for Men

Designed by Jennifer Ghionzoli

Compiled and edited by Amy E. Mason. All rights reserved.

Scripture quotations are taken from the *Holy Bible,* New Living Translation, copyright © 1996, 2004, 2007 by Tyndale House Foundation. Used by permission of Tyndale House Publishers, Inc., Carol Stream, Illinois 60188. All rights reserved.

ISBN 978-1-4143-6487-2

Printed in the United States of America

18   17   16   15   14   13   12
7   6   5   4   3   2   1

❦ CONTENTS ❧

Small things often make the greatest impact. This book of Bible promises is small in size but will hopefully become one of your most treasured resources for hope and encouragement. Life is full of twists and surprises—some good and some bad. As we experience life day by day, month by month, and year by year, we face many hurts, doubts, and problems. We have questions about what to do next, where to go, and why things happen the way they do. Life doesn't always work according to plan.

So how do we keep moving forward with a positive attitude, hope, and a spirit of joy in spite of the bumps along the way? This little book can help you make sense of today's challenges. Knowing God's promises will give you confident peace and security in the midst of confusing and chaotic circumstances. When you have questions, doubts, or fears, this book can be a wonderful resource to come back to again and again.

Thankfully, God keeps all his promises. This makes his Word, the Bible, the greatest of treasures, because it is filled with promises you know will be kept. These are assurances God makes not only to his people in general but to you personally. One of God's greatest promises is that his Word will last forever (Isaiah 40:8; Matthew 24:35; 1 Peter 1:23-25), which means his promises will also stand for eternity. Though human promises often fail and disappoint us, God's commitments fulfill and sustain us by providing guidance, teaching, encouragement, forgiveness, joy, and the confidence that the future is secure.

This little book is packed full of God's greatest and most personal promises—more than 400 promises covering more than 80 different topics. They have been carefully selected to speak to some of the unique topics and issues men face. All of the passages are drawn from the New Living Translation of the Bible, the most readable and accurate translation available today. The topics selected in this book cover different seasons and walks of life to show that God's care and concern extend to all people for all time, including you! His promises are relevant in your most needy hour, as well as in your times of blessing and in the routine of daily life. Knowing God's promises will help you discover what God desires for your life and how to receive and enjoy all that God has in store for you.

⌑ ABILITIES

When your abilities seem limited . . .

He takes no pleasure in the strength of a horse or in human might. No, the LORD's delight is in those who fear him, those who put their hope in his unfailing love.

Psalm 147:10-11

Well done, my good and faithful servant. You have been faithful in handling this small amount, so now I will give you many more responsibilities.

Matthew 25:21

When you are jealous of someone else's skills . . .

In his grace, God has given us different gifts for doing certain things well.

Romans 12:6

When you question your ability to serve God . . .

Work hard to show the results of your salvation, obeying God with deep reverence and fear. For God is working in you, giving you the desire and the power to do what pleases him.
Philippians 2:12-13

ABSENCE

When God seems far away . . .

Be sure of this: I am with you always, even to the end of the age.
Matthew 28:20

When people fail to be there for you . . .

I can never escape from your Spirit! I can never get away from your presence! If I go up to heaven, you are there; if I go down to the grave, you are there. If I ride the wings of the morning, if I dwell by the farthest oceans, even there your hand will guide me, and your strength will support me.
Psalm 139:7-10

ACCOUNTABILITY

When you need support as you try to walk in God's ways . . .

Two people are better off than one, for they can help each other succeed. If one person falls, the other can reach out and help. But someone who falls alone is in real trouble. Likewise, two people lying close together can keep each other warm. But how can one be warm alone? A person standing alone can be attacked and defeated, but two can stand back-to-back and conquer. Three are even better, for a triple-braided cord is not easily broken.

Ecclesiastes 4:9-12

Confess your sins to each other and pray for each other so that you may be healed. The earnest prayer of a righteous person has great power and produces wonderful results.

James 5:16

When searching for trustworthy advisors . . .

Oh, the joys of those who do not follow the advice of the wicked, or stand around with sinners, or join in with mockers.

Psalm 1:1

When you are aware of God's presence with you . . .

I, the LORD, search all hearts and examine secret motives. I give all people their due rewards, according to what their actions deserve.

Jeremiah 17:10

ANGER

When anger wells up inside you . . .

Stop being angry! Turn from your rage! Do not lose your temper—it only leads to harm.

Psalm 37:8

A gentle answer deflects anger, but harsh words make tempers flare.

Proverbs 15:1

Sensible people control their temper; they earn respect by overlooking wrongs.

Proverbs 19:11

When you need an outlet for your anger . . .

Morning, noon, and night I cry out in my distress, and the LORD hears my voice.

Psalm 55:17

When you feel your anger is justified . . .

God called you to do good, even if it means suffering, just as Christ suffered for you. He is your example, and you must follow in his steps. . . . He did not retaliate when he was insulted, nor threaten revenge when he suffered. He left his case in the hands of God, who always judges fairly.

1 Peter 2:21, 23

When you feel the enemy is raging around you . . .

Mightier than the violent raging of the seas, mightier than the breakers on the shore—the LORD above is mightier than these! Your royal laws cannot be changed. Your reign, O LORD, is holy forever and ever.

Psalm 93:4-5

When God seems angry with you . . .

His anger lasts only a moment, but his favor lasts a lifetime! Weeping may last through the night, but joy comes with the morning.

Psalm 30:5

I hear the tumult of the raging seas as your waves and surging tides sweep over me. But each day the LORD pours his unfailing love upon me, and through each night I sing his songs, praying to God who gives life.

Psalm 42:7-8

APATHY

When you've lost your enthusiasm for the Lord . . .

I will give them singleness of heart and put a new spirit
within them. I will take away their stony, stubborn heart and
give them a tender, responsive heart, so they will obey my
decrees and regulations. Then they will truly be my people,
and I will be their God.

Ezekiel 11:19-20

When you don't even know what you want anymore . . .

Take delight in the LORD, and he will give you your heart's
desires.

Psalm 37:4

ATTITUDE

When you want your attitude to be pleasing to God . . .

God blesses those who are poor and realize their need for him,
for the Kingdom of Heaven is theirs. . . . God blesses those
who are humble, for they will inherit the whole earth. . . .
God blesses those whose hearts are pure, for they will see God.

Matthew 5:3, 5, 8

When you are fighting a bad attitude . . .

A cheerful heart is good medicine, but a broken spirit saps
a person's strength.

Proverbs 17:22

Haughtiness goes before destruction; humility precedes
honor.

Proverbs 18:12

I have learned how to be content with whatever I have. I know how to live on almost nothing or with everything. I have learned the secret of living in every situation, whether it is with a full stomach or empty, with plenty or little. For I can do everything through Christ, who gives me strength.

Philippians 4:11-13

BACKSLIDING

When you want to grow in your obedience to God . . .

Be careful. Don't let your heart be deceived so that you turn away from the LORD and serve and worship other gods. If you do, the LORD's anger will burn against you.

Deuteronomy 11:16-17

Keep watch and pray, so that you will not give in to temptation. For the spirit is willing, but the body is weak!

Matthew 26:41

BEGINNINGS

When you want this day to be different . . .

Great is his faithfulness; his mercies begin afresh each morning.

Lamentations 3:23

When you wish you could start over . . .

This means that anyone who belongs to Christ has become a new person. The old life is gone; a new life has begun!

2 Corinthians 5:17

When God begins to work in your heart . . .

I am certain that God, who began the good work within you, will continue his work until it is finally finished on the day when Christ Jesus returns.

Philippians 1:6

BIBLE

When you need a lesson in the truth . . .

All Scripture is inspired by God and is useful to teach us what is true and to make us realize what is wrong in our lives. It corrects us when we are wrong and teaches us to do what is right.

2 Timothy 3:16

When you need to be strengthened . . .

Your promise revives me; it comforts me in all my troubles.

Psalm 119:50

When I discovered your words, I devoured them. They are my joy and my heart's delight, for I bear your name, O LORD God of Heaven's Armies.

Jeremiah 15:16

When you wonder if the Bible is trustworthy . . .

Not one word has failed of all the wonderful promises he gave through his servant Moses.

1 Kings 8:56

God's way is perfect. All the LORD's promises prove true.

Psalm 18:30

The laws of the LORD are true; each one is fair. They are more desirable than gold, even the finest gold. They are sweeter than honey, even honey dripping from the comb. They are a warning to your servant, a great reward for those who obey them.

Psalm 19:9-11

When you wonder if the Bible applies to your life today . . .

I know his commands lead to eternal life.

John 12:50

The word of God is alive and powerful. It is sharper than the sharpest two-edged sword, cutting between soul and spirit, between joint and marrow. It exposes our innermost thoughts and desires.

Hebrews 4:12

CALL OF GOD

When you wonder if God is calling you to serve him . . .

A spiritual gift is given to each of us so we can help each other.

1 Corinthians 12:7

May the God of peace make you holy in every way, and may your whole spirit and soul and body be kept blameless until our Lord Jesus Christ comes again. God will make this happen, for he who calls you is faithful.

1 Thessalonians 5:23-24

When you fear your mistakes disqualify you from your calling . . .

Many of the people of Israel are now enemies of the Good News, and this benefits you Gentiles. Yet they are still the people he loves because he chose their ancestors Abraham, Isaac, and Jacob. For God's gifts and his call can never be withdrawn.

Romans 11:28-29

CHALLENGES

When you need help in facing your challenges . . .

Commit everything you do to the LORD. Trust him, and he will help you.

Psalm 37:5

Give all your worries and cares to God, for he cares about you.

1 Peter 5:7

When challenges come out of the blue . . .

God is our refuge and strength, always ready to help in times of trouble.

Psalm 46:1

CHANGE

When good things come to an end . . .

The grass withers and the flowers fade, but the word of our God stands forever.

Isaiah 40:8

Heaven and earth will disappear, but my words will never disappear.
Mark 13:31

When people change . . .

God is not a man, so he does not lie. He is not human, so he does not change his mind. Has he ever spoken and failed to act? Has he ever promised and not carried it through?
Numbers 23:19

I am the LORD, and I do not change.
Malachi 3:6

When you long for stability . . .

LORD, you remain the same forever! Your throne continues from generation to generation.
Lamentations 5:19

Jesus Christ is the same yesterday, today, and forever.
Hebrews 13:8

CHARACTER

When you think about who you want to become . . .

Because of his glory and excellence, he has given us great and precious promises. These are the promises that enable you to share his divine nature and escape the world's corruption caused by human desires. In view of all this, make every effort to respond to God's promises. . . . The more you grow like this, the more productive and useful you will be in your knowledge of our Lord Jesus Christ.
2 Peter 1:4-5, 8

When you wonder about the worth of developing godly character . . .

Dear brothers and sisters, work hard to prove that you really are among those God has called and chosen. Do these things, and you will never fall away. Then God will give you a grand entrance into the eternal Kingdom of our Lord and Savior Jesus Christ.

2 Peter 1:10-11

CHILDREN

When you are frustrated with your children . . .

Children are a gift from the LORD; they are a reward from him.

Psalm 127:3

When you wonder how to teach your children about God . . .

Commit yourselves wholeheartedly to these words of mine. Tie them to your hands and wear them on your forehead as reminders. Teach them to your children. Talk about them when you are at home and when you are on the road, when you are going to bed and when you are getting up. Write them on the doorposts of your house and on your gates, so that as long as the sky remains above the earth, you and your children may flourish.

Deuteronomy 11:18-21

Believe in the Lord Jesus and you will be saved, along with everyone in your household.

Acts 16:31

When you can't be there to protect your children . . .

I will pour out my Spirit on your descendants, and my blessing on your children.
Isaiah 44:3

My Spirit will not leave them, and neither will these words I have given you. They will be on your lips and on the lips of your children and your children's children forever. I, the LORD, have spoken!
Isaiah 59:21

When you wish to see your children as Jesus does . . .

[Jesus] said to them, "Let the children come to me. Don't stop them! For the Kingdom of God belongs to those who are like these children. I tell you the truth, anyone who doesn't receive the Kingdom of God like a child will never enter it."
Mark 10:14-15

CHOICES

When you come to a fork in the road . . .

Understand what it means to fear the LORD, and you will gain knowledge of God. . . . He guards the paths of the just and protects those who are faithful to him. Then you will understand what is right, just, and fair, and you will find the right way to go. For wisdom will enter your heart, and knowledge will fill you with joy. Wise choices will watch over you. Understanding will keep you safe.
Proverbs 2:5, 8-11

When you've exhausted all your options and need insight from somewhere else . . .

Trust in the LORD with all your heart; do not depend on your own understanding. Seek his will in all you do, and he will show you which path to take.

Proverbs 3:5-6

CHURCH

When you wonder if you're needed at church . . .

Just as our bodies have many parts and each part has a special function, so it is with Christ's body. We are many parts of one body, and we all belong to each other.

Romans 12:4-5

When you feel like skipping regular church attendance . . .

Let us not neglect our meeting together, as some people do, but encourage one another, especially now that the day of his return is drawing near.

Hebrews 10:25

When you wish you could see Jesus at work in the world today . . .

It is the LORD who provides the sun to light the day and the moon and stars to light the night, and who stirs the sea into roaring waves. His name is the LORD of Heaven's Armies.

Jeremiah 31:35

God has put all things under the authority of Christ and has made him head over all things for the benefit of the church. And the church is his body; it is made full and complete by Christ, who fills all things everywhere with himself.

Ephesians 1:22-23

God is working in you, giving you the desire and the power to do what pleases him.

Philippians 2:13

COMMITMENT

When you dedicate your life to God . . .

Commit everything you do to the LORD. Trust him, and he will help you.

Psalm 37:5

Now you must give yourselves to be slaves to righteous living so that you will become holy. . . . Now you do those things that lead to holiness and result in eternal life. For the wages of sin is death, but the free gift of God is eternal life through Christ Jesus our Lord.

Romans 6:19, 22-23

When you question God's commitment to you . . .

The Lord is faithful; he will strengthen you and guard you from the evil one.

2 Thessalonians 3:3

When counting the cost of commitment to God . . .

If we are faithful to the end, trusting God just as firmly as when we first believed, we will share in all that belongs to Christ.

Hebrews 3:14

CONDEMNATION

When you fear that God will abandon you because of your sin . . .

There is no condemnation for those who belong to Christ Jesus. And because you belong to him, the power of the life-giving Spirit has freed you from the power of sin that leads to death.
  Romans 8:1-2

When you feel constantly accused . . .

What shall we say about such wonderful things as these? If God is for us, who can ever be against us? . . . Who dares accuse us whom God has chosen for his own? No one—for God himself has given us right standing with himself. Who then will condemn us? No one—for Christ Jesus died for us and was raised to life for us, and he is sitting in the place of honor at God's right hand, pleading for us.
  Romans 8:31, 33-34

Even if we feel guilty, God is greater than our feelings, and he knows everything.
  1 John 3:20

CONFESSION

When you'd rather keep your mistakes hidden . . .

If we confess our sins to him, he is faithful and just to forgive us our sins and to cleanse us from all wickedness.
  1 John 1:9

When you wonder if confessing sin does any good . . .

People who conceal their sins will not prosper, but if they confess and turn from them, they will receive mercy. Blessed are those who fear to do wrong, but the stubborn are headed for serious trouble.

Proverbs 28:13-14

When you acknowledge that Jesus is your Savior . . .

If you confess with your mouth that Jesus is Lord and believe in your heart that God raised him from the dead, you will be saved.

Romans 10:9

CONFIDENCE

When you need confidence in the direction of your life . . .

The LORD keeps watch over you as you come and go, both now and forever.

Psalm 121:8

When you aren't sure that God is able . . .

If we are thrown into the blazing furnace, the God whom we serve is able to save us. He will rescue us from your power, Your Majesty.

Daniel 3:17

I can do everything through Christ, who gives me strength.

Philippians 4:13

When you need confidence to live without fear . . .

Those who are righteous will be long remembered. They do not fear bad news; they confidently trust the LORD to care for them. They are confident and fearless and can face their foes triumphantly.

Psalm 112:6-8

⟪ COURAGE

When you feel weak and vulnerable . . .

Be strong and courageous! Do not be afraid and do not panic before them. For the LORD your God will personally go ahead of you. He will neither fail you nor abandon you.

Deuteronomy 31:6

When you feel discouraged . . .

This is my command—be strong and courageous! Do not be afraid or discouraged. For the LORD your God is with you wherever you go.

Joshua 1:9

As soon as I pray, you answer me; you encourage me by giving me strength.

Psalm 138:3

When you need courage while enduring the blows of life . . .

The LORD is my strength and shield. I trust him with all my heart. He helps me, and my heart is filled with joy. I burst out in songs of thanksgiving.

Psalm 28:7

When you need courage to stand up for your faith . . .

You will receive power when the Holy Spirit comes upon you. And you will be my witnesses, telling people about me everywhere . . . to the ends of the earth.

Acts 1:8

I am not ashamed of this Good News about Christ. It is the power of God at work, saving everyone who believes— the Jew first and also the Gentile.

Romans 1:16

The Spirit who lives in you is greater than the spirit who lives in the world.

1 John 4:4

DEATH

When life seems so short . . .

My health may fail, and my spirit may grow weak, but God remains the strength of my heart; he is mine forever.

Psalm 73:26

When you've lost someone you love . . .

The LORD cares deeply when his loved ones die.

Psalm 116:15

He heals the brokenhearted and bandages their wounds.

Psalm 147:3

God blesses those who mourn, for they will be comforted.

Matthew 5:4

When you need the strength to face death . . .

Jesus told her, "I am the resurrection and the life. Anyone who believes in me will live, even after dying."

John 11:25

Christ lives within you, so even though your body will die because of sin, the Spirit gives you life because you have been made right with God. The Spirit of God, who raised Jesus from the dead, lives in you. And just as God raised Christ Jesus from the dead, he will give life to your mortal bodies by this same Spirit living within you.

Romans 8:10-11

When our dying bodies have been transformed into bodies that will never die, this Scripture will be fulfilled: "Death is swallowed up in victory." . . . But thank God! He gives us victory over sin and death through our Lord Jesus Christ.

1 Corinthians 15:54, 57

When you need assurance of heaven . . .

We are always confident, even though we know that as long as we live in these bodies we are not at home with the Lord. For we live by believing and not by seeing. Yes, we are fully confident, and we would rather be away from these earthly bodies, for then we will be at home with the Lord. So whether we are here in this body or away from this body, our goal is to please him.

2 Corinthians 5:6-9

DESIRES

When your desires go unsatisfied . . .

The LORD says, "I will guide you along the best pathway for your life."

Psalm 32:8

You know what I long for, Lord; you hear my every sigh.

Psalm 38:9

When you are fighting wrong desires . . .

Guard your heart above all else, for it determines the course
of your life.

   Proverbs 4:23

Don't copy the behavior and customs of this world, but let
God transform you into a new person by changing the way
you think. Then you will learn to know God's will for you,
which is good and pleasing and perfect.

   Romans 12:2

DISCERNMENT

When you need spiritual direction . . .

Your word is a lamp to guide my feet and a light for my path.

   Psalm 119:105

Give discernment to me, your servant; then I will understand
your laws.

   Psalm 119:125

When you want to know what the Lord thinks . . .

We have received God's Spirit (not the world's spirit), so
we can know the wonderful things God has freely given
us. . . . We speak words given to us by the Spirit, using the
Spirit's words to explain spiritual truths. But people who
aren't spiritual can't receive these truths from God's Spirit.
It all sounds foolish to them and they can't understand it, for
only those who are spiritual can understand what the Spirit
means. . . . But we understand these things, for we have the
mind of Christ.

   1 Corinthians 2:12-14, 16

DISTRACTIONS

When your spiritual life keeps getting sidetracked . . .

Our great desire is that you will keep on loving others as long as life lasts, in order to make certain that what you hope for will come true. Then you will not become spiritually dull and indifferent. Instead, you will follow the example of those who are going to inherit God's promises because of their faith and endurance.

Hebrews 6:11-12

Let us strip off every weight that slows us down, especially the sin that so easily trips us up. And let us run with endurance the race God has set before us. We do this by keeping our eyes on Jesus, the champion who initiates and perfects our faith.

Hebrews 12:1-2

DOUBT

When you question God's care for you . . .

Not a single sparrow can fall to the ground without your Father knowing it. . . . Don't be afraid; you are more valuable to God than a whole flock of sparrows.

Matthew 10:29, 31

Seek the Kingdom of God above all else, and he will give you everything you need. So don't be afraid, little flock. For it gives your Father great happiness to give you the Kingdom.

Luke 12:31-32

Be satisfied with what you have. For God has said, "I will never fail you. I will never abandon you."

Hebrews 13:5

When you doubt your testimony will make a difference . . .

Faith comes from hearing, that is, hearing the Good News about Christ.

Romans 10:17

The Holy Spirit produces this kind of fruit in our lives: love, joy, peace, patience, kindness, goodness, faithfulness, gentleness, and self-control.

Galatians 5:22-23

When you question what God can do . . .

"What do you mean, 'If I can'?" Jesus asked. "Anything is possible if a person believes."

Mark 9:23

When obstacles cause you to lose heart . . .

Jesus told them, "I tell you the truth, if you have faith and don't doubt, you can do things like this and much more. You can even say to this mountain, 'May you be lifted up and thrown into the sea,' and it will happen. You can pray for anything, and if you have faith, you will receive it."

Matthew 21:21-22

ENCOURAGEMENT

When you need confidence in the midst of frustrating circumstances . . .

We can rejoice, too, when we run into problems and trials, for we know that they help us develop endurance. And endurance develops strength of character, and character strengthens our confident hope of salvation. And this hope will not lead to disappointment. For we know how dearly God loves us, because he has given us the Holy Spirit to fill our hearts with his love.

Romans 5:3-5

Dear brothers and sisters, be patient as you wait for the Lord's return. Consider the farmers who patiently wait for the rains in the fall and in the spring. They eagerly look for the valuable harvest to ripen. You, too, must be patient. Take courage, for the coming of the Lord is near.

James 5:7-8

When you want to be an encouragement to others . . .

A cheerful look brings joy to the heart; good news makes for good health.

Proverbs 15:30

We have been greatly encouraged in the midst of our troubles and suffering, dear brothers and sisters, because you have remained strong in your faith. It gives us new life to know that you are standing firm in the Lord.

1 Thessalonians 3:7-8

ENDURANCE

When you persevere in doing what is right . . .

Let's not get tired of doing what is good. At just the right time we will reap a harvest of blessing if we don't give up.

Galatians 6:9

When you endure hardship . . .

I am willing to endure anything if it will bring salvation and eternal glory in Christ Jesus to those God has chosen. This is a trustworthy saying: If we die with him, we will also live with him. If we endure hardship, we will reign with him. If we deny him, he will deny us.

2 Timothy 2:10-12

When your endurance is being tested . . .

Dear brothers and sisters, when troubles come your way, consider it an opportunity for great joy. For you know that when your faith is tested, your endurance has a chance to grow. So let it grow, for when your endurance is fully developed, you will be perfect and complete, needing nothing.

James 1:2-4

When you start to lose patience with your circumstances . . .

God blesses those who patiently endure testing and temptation. Afterward they will receive the crown of life that God has promised to those who love him.

James 1:12

FORGIVENESS

When you're in need of forgiveness . . .

There is forgiveness of sins for all who repent.

Luke 24:47

Everyone has sinned; we all fall short of God's glorious standard. Yet God, with undeserved kindness, declares that we are righteous. He did this through Christ Jesus when he freed us from the penalty for our sins. For God presented Jesus as the sacrifice for sin.

Romans 3:23-25

Let us come boldly to the throne of our gracious God. There we will receive his mercy, and we will find grace to help us when we need it most.

Hebrews 4:16

When you're truly sorry for your sin . . .

The sacrifice you desire is a broken spirit. You will not reject a broken and repentant heart, O God.
  Psalm 51:17

"Come now, let's settle this," says the LORD. "Though your sins are like scarlet, I will make them as white as snow. Though they are red like crimson, I will make them as white as wool."
  Isaiah 1:18

If we confess our sins to him, he is faithful and just to forgive us our sins and to cleanse us from all wickedness.
  1 John 1:9

When you wonder how forgiveness is possible . . .

[Jesus said,] "This is my blood, which confirms the covenant between God and his people. It is poured out as a sacrifice to forgive the sins of many."
  Matthew 26:28

Brothers, listen! We are here to proclaim that through this man Jesus there is forgiveness for your sins.
  Acts 13:38

When guilt continues to haunt you . . .

God, with undeserved kindness, declares that we are righteous. He did this through Christ Jesus when he freed us from the penalty for our sins.
  Romans 3:24

When you remain angry with someone who has wronged you . . .

Make allowance for each other's faults, and forgive anyone who offends you. Remember, the Lord forgave you, so you must forgive others.

Colossians 3:13

GENEROSITY

When you are thinking about giving help to the needy . . .

Give generously to the poor, not grudgingly, for the LORD your God will bless you in everything you do.

Deuteronomy 15:10

Then these righteous ones will reply, "Lord, when did we ever see you hungry and feed you? Or thirsty and give you something to drink? Or a stranger and show you hospitality? Or naked and give you clothing? When did we ever see you sick or in prison and visit you?" And the King will say, "I tell you the truth, when you did it to one of the least of these my brothers and sisters, you were doing it to me!"

Matthew 25:37-40

When you're willing to give the Lord everything . . .

Everyone who has given up houses or brothers or sisters or father or mother or children or property, for my sake, will receive a hundred times as much in return and will inherit eternal life.

Matthew 19:29

When you wrestle with how much to give . . .

Give in proportion to what you have. Whatever you give is acceptable if you give it eagerly.

2 Corinthians 8:11-12

You must each decide in your heart how much to give. And don't give reluctantly or in response to pressure. "For God loves a person who gives cheerfully." And God will generously provide all you need. Then you will always have everything you need and plenty left over to share with others.

2 Corinthians 9:7-8

When you'd rather get than give . . .

Give, and you will receive. Your gift will return to you in full—pressed down, shaken together to make room for more, running over, and poured into your lap. The amount you give will determine the amount you get back.

Luke 6:38

HEAVEN

When you want to be sure where you go when you die . . .

Jesus told her, "I am the resurrection and the life. Anyone who believes in me will live, even after dying. Everyone who lives in me and believes in me will never ever die."

John 11:25-26

When you long for your heavenly home . . .

Surely your goodness and unfailing love will pursue me all the days of my life, and I will live in the house of the LORD forever.

Psalm 23:6

You must remain faithful to what you have been taught from the beginning. If you do, you will remain in fellowship with the Son and with the Father. And in this fellowship we enjoy the eternal life he promised us.

1 John 2:24-25

HOLY SPIRIT

When nothing in your life seems sacred . . .

Don't you realize that your body is the temple of the Holy Spirit, who lives in you and was given to you by God? You do not belong to yourself, for God bought you with a high price. So you must honor God with your body.

1 Corinthians 6:19-20

When you need a spiritual guarantee . . .

The Spirit is God's guarantee that he will give us the inheritance he promised and that he has purchased us to be his own people. He did this so we would praise and glorify him.

Ephesians 1:14

When you want to know if the Holy Spirit lives in you . . .

Peter replied, "Each of you must repent of your sins and turn to God, and be baptized in the name of Jesus Christ for the forgiveness of your sins. Then you will receive the gift of the Holy Spirit. This promise is to you, and to your children, and even to the Gentiles—all who have been called by the Lord our God."

Acts 2:38-39

Those who obey God's commandments remain in fellowship with him, and he with them. And we know he lives in us because the Spirit he gave us lives in us.

1 John 3:24

When you want to know the role of the Holy Spirit in your life . . .

I will send you the Advocate—the Spirit of truth. He will come to you from the Father and will testify all about me.

John 15:26

When the Spirit of truth comes, he will guide you into all truth. He will not speak on his own but will tell you what he has heard. He will tell you about the future.

John 16:13

You have not received a spirit that makes you fearful slaves. Instead, you received God's Spirit when he adopted you as his own children. Now we call him, "Abba, Father."

Romans 8:15

We have received God's Spirit (not the world's spirit), so we can know the wonderful things God has freely given us.

1 Corinthians 2:12

HUMILITY

When you want to be the greatest . . .

Anyone who becomes as humble as this little child is the greatest in the Kingdom of Heaven.

Matthew 18:4

When you think you deserve all the credit . . .

He leads the humble in doing right, teaching them his way.

Psalm 25:9

Though the LORD is great, he cares for the humble, but he keeps his distance from the proud.

Psalm 138:6

I live in the high and holy place with those whose spirits are contrite and humble. I restore the crushed spirit of the humble and revive the courage of those with repentant hearts.

Isaiah 57:15

What do you have that God hasn't given you? And if everything you have is from God, why boast as though it were not a gift?

1 Corinthians 4:7

When you wonder if humility will be rewarded . . .

The LORD supports the humble.

Psalm 147:6

The LORD delights in his people; he crowns the humble with victory.

Psalm 149:4

The humble will be filled with fresh joy from the LORD.

Isaiah 29:19

IMPOSSIBLE

When there seems no way out . . .

Nothing is impossible with God.

Luke 1:37

All glory to God, who is able, through his mighty power at work within us, to accomplish infinitely more than we might ask or think.

Ephesians 3:20

When you need a miracle . . .

You faithfully answer our prayers with awesome deeds, O God our savior. You are the hope of everyone on earth.
Psalm 65:5

Who can list the glorious miracles of the LORD? Who can ever praise him enough?
Psalm 106:2

INTEGRITY

When you want to set an example for others . . .

The LORD rewarded me for doing right. . . . To the faithful you show yourself faithful; to those with integrity you show integrity.
Psalm 18:24-25

If you are faithful in little things, you will be faithful in large ones. But if you are dishonest in little things, you won't be honest with greater responsibilities.
Luke 16:10

If you keep yourself pure, you will be a special utensil for honorable use. Your life will be clean, and you will be ready for the Master to use you for every good work.
2 Timothy 2:21

When you are tempted to give in just a little . . .

People with integrity walk safely, but those who follow crooked paths will slip and fall.
Proverbs 10:9

Be careful to live properly among your unbelieving neighbors. Then even if they accuse you of doing wrong, they will see your honorable behavior, and they will give honor to God when he judges the world.

1 Peter 2:12

When you need help living a godly life . . .

My child, listen to what I say, and treasure my commands. Tune your ears to wisdom, and concentrate on understanding. . . . Then you will understand what it means to fear the LORD, and you will gain knowledge of God. . . . Then you will understand what is right, just, and fair, and you will find the right way to go.

Proverbs 2:1-2, 5, 9

Fools think their own way is right, but the wise listen to others.

Proverbs 12:15

Confess your sins to each other and pray for each other.

James 5:16

JESUS CHRIST

When you want to know more about him . . .

God promised this Good News long ago through his prophets in the holy Scriptures. The Good News is about his Son.

Romans 1:2-3

When you want to become his follower . . .

If you confess with your mouth that Jesus is Lord and believe in your heart that God raised him from the dead, you will be saved.

Romans 10:9

When you doubt Jesus is the only way to heaven . . .

Jesus told him, "I am the way, the truth, and the life. No one can come to the Father except through me."
John 14:6

For there is only one God and one Mediator who can reconcile God and humanity—the man Christ Jesus.
1 Timothy 2:5

When believing in Christ alone seems narrow-minded . . .

God loved the world so much that he gave his one and only Son, so that everyone who believes in him will not perish but have eternal life. God sent his Son into the world not to judge the world, but to save the world through him.
John 3:16-17

JUSTICE

When God doesn't seem fair . . .

Then at last everyone will say, "There truly is a reward for those who live for God; surely there is a God who judges justly here on earth."
Psalm 58:11

When you want to bring justice on those who offend you . . .

Dear friends, never take revenge. Leave that to the righteous anger of God. For the Scriptures say, "I will take revenge; I will pay them back," says the LORD.
Romans 12:19

In his justice he will pay back those who persecute you.
2 Thessalonians 1:6

When you fight for the disadvantaged and the poor . . .

God blesses those who hunger and thirst for justice, for they will be satisfied.
Matthew 5:6

LEADERSHIP

When you need a leader for all of life . . .

The LORD is good and does what is right; he shows the proper path to those who go astray. He leads the humble in doing right, teaching them his way. The LORD leads with unfailing love and faithfulness all who keep his covenant and obey his demands.
Psalm 25:8-10

When you want to be a great leader . . .

Even the Son of Man came not to be served but to serve others and to give his life as a ransom for many.
Matthew 20:28

LEGACY

When you walk in God's ways . . .

You guide me with your counsel, leading me to a glorious destiny.
Psalm 73:24

When you want to build something that will last . . .

Because of God's grace to me, I have laid the foundation like
an expert builder. Now others are building on it. But whoever
is building on this foundation must be very careful. For no
one can lay any foundation other than the one we already
have—Jesus Christ.

1 Corinthians 3:10-11

When you want to leave behind a spiritual heritage . . .

Praise the LORD! How joyful are those who fear the LORD
and delight in obeying his commands. Their children will be
successful everywhere; an entire generation of godly people
will be blessed. They themselves will be wealthy, and their
good deeds will last forever.

Psalm 112:1-3

The godly walk with integrity; blessed are their children who
follow them.

Proverbs 20:7

LOVE

When you wonder what real love looks like . . .

Love is patient and kind. Love is not jealous or boastful or
proud or rude. It does not demand its own way. It is not
irritable, and it keeps no record of being wronged. It does not
rejoice about injustice but rejoices whenever the truth wins
out. Love never gives up, never loses faith, is always hopeful,
and endures through every circumstance.

1 Corinthians 13:4-7

This is real love—not that we loved God, but that he loved
us and sent his Son as a sacrifice to take away our sins.

1 John 4:10

When your love for others is halfhearted . . .

You were cleansed from your sins when you obeyed the truth,
so now you must show sincere love to each other as brothers
and sisters. Love each other deeply with all your heart.

   1 Peter 1:22

As we live in God, our love grows more perfect. So we will
not be afraid on the day of judgment, but we can face him
with confidence because we live like Jesus here in this world.
Such love has no fear, because perfect love expels all fear. If
we are afraid, it is for fear of punishment, and this shows that
we have not fully experienced his perfect love. We love each
other because he loved us first.

   1 John 4:17-19

LOVE OF GOD

When you wonder if God loves you . . .

I will be glad and rejoice in your unfailing love, for you have
seen my troubles, and you care about the anguish of my soul.

   Psalm 31:7

The LORD is compassionate and merciful, slow to get angry
and filled with unfailing love.

   Psalm 103:8

When you want to continually experience God's love . . .

I have loved you even as the Father has loved me. Remain in
my love. When you obey my commandments, you remain
in my love, just as I obey my Father's commandments and
remain in his love.

   John 15:9-10

I am in them and you are in me. May they experience such perfect unity that the world will know that you sent me and that you love them as much as you love me.

John 17:23

When you feel far from the reach of God's love . . .

I am convinced that nothing can ever separate us from God's love. Neither death nor life, neither angels nor demons, neither our fears for today nor our worries about tomorrow—not even the powers of hell can separate us from God's love. No power in the sky above or in the earth below—indeed, nothing in all creation will ever be able to separate us from the love of God that is revealed in Christ Jesus our Lord.

Romans 8:38-39

MATURITY

When you want to be known as a man of godly character . . .

Blessed are those who trust in the LORD and have made the LORD their hope and confidence. They are like trees planted along a riverbank, with roots that reach deep into the water. Such trees are not bothered by the heat or worried by long months of drought. Their leaves stay green, and they never stop producing fruit.

Jeremiah 17:7-8

All of us who have had that veil removed can see and reflect the glory of the Lord. And the Lord—who is the Spirit—makes us more and more like him as we are changed into his glorious image.

2 Corinthians 3:18

When you pursue righteousness . . .

The way of the righteous is like the first gleam of dawn,
which shines ever brighter until the full light of day.
  Proverbs 4:18

MEDITATION

When you want to connect with God . . .

I wait quietly before God, for my victory comes from him.
. . . Let all that I am wait quietly before God, for my hope
is in him.
  Psalm 62:1, 5

Those who are dominated by the sinful nature think about
sinful things, but those who are controlled by the Holy Spirit
think about things that please the Spirit.
  Romans 8:5

MERCY

When you fear God's punishment . . .

Return to the LORD your God, for he is merciful and
compassionate, slow to get angry and filled with unfailing
love. He is eager to relent and not punish.
  Joel 2:13

When you wonder about the extent of God's mercy . . .

He shows mercy from generation to generation to all who
fear him.
  Luke 1:50

God is so rich in mercy, and he loved us so much, that even though we were dead because of our sins, he gave us life when he raised Christ from the dead. (It is only by God's grace that you have been saved!)

Ephesians 2:4-5

When you want God to be merciful to you . . .

God blesses those who are merciful, for they will be shown mercy.

Matthew 5:7

When you want to reflect on God's great mercy toward you . . .

God is so rich in mercy . . . he raised us from the dead along with Christ and seated us with him in the heavenly realms because we are united with Christ Jesus. So God can point to us in all future ages as examples of the incredible wealth of his grace and kindness toward us, as shown in all he has done for us who are united with Christ Jesus.

Ephesians 2:4, 6-7

When God our Savior revealed his kindness and love, he saved us, not because of the righteous things we had done, but because of his mercy. He washed away our sins, giving us a new birth and new life through the Holy Spirit. He generously poured out the Spirit upon us through Jesus Christ our Savior. Because of his grace he declared us righteous and gave us confidence that we will inherit eternal life.

Titus 3:4-7

MONEY

When money becomes an idol . . .

Remember the LORD your God. He is the one who gives you power to be successful, in order to fulfill the covenant he confirmed to your ancestors with an oath.
Deuteronomy 8:18

No one can serve two masters. For you will hate one and love the other; you will be devoted to one and despise the other. You cannot serve both God and money.
Matthew 6:24

Don't love money; be satisfied with what you have. For God has said, "I will never fail you. I will never abandon you."
Hebrews 13:5

When it seems there is never enough . . .

Don't wear yourself out trying to get rich. Be wise enough to know when to quit. In the blink of an eye wealth disappears, for it will sprout wings and fly away like an eagle.
Proverbs 23:4-5

When you want to invest for the future . . .

Don't store up treasures here on earth, where moths eat them and rust destroys them, and where thieves break in and steal. Store your treasures in heaven, where moths and rust cannot destroy, and thieves do not break in and steal. Wherever your treasure is, there the desires of your heart will also be.
Matthew 6:19-21

Teach those who are rich in this world not to be proud and not to trust in their money, which is so unreliable. Their trust should be in God, who richly gives us all we need for our enjoyment. Tell them to use their money to do good. They should be rich in good works and generous to those in need, always being ready to share with others. By doing this they will be storing up their treasure as a good foundation for the future so that they may experience true life.

1 Timothy 6:17-19

NEEDS

When there's not enough to go around . . .

This same God who takes care of me will supply all your needs from his glorious riches, which have been given to us in Christ Jesus.

Philippians 4:19

When the task exceeds your abilities and resources . . .

By his divine power, God has given us everything we need for living a godly life. We have received all of this by coming to know him, the one who called us to himself by means of his marvelous glory and excellence.

2 Peter 1:3

OBEDIENCE

When you want the benefits of obedience . . .

Joyful are those who obey his laws and search for him with all their hearts.

Psalm 119:2

If you love me, obey my commandments. And I will ask the Father, and he will give you another Advocate, who will never leave you.
John 14:15-16

Those who obey God's commandments remain in fellowship with him, and he with them. And we know he lives in us because the Spirit he gave us lives in us.
1 John 3:24

When your obedience is halfhearted . . .

If you ignore the least commandment and teach others to do the same, you will be called the least in the Kingdom of Heaven. But anyone who obeys God's laws and teaches them will be called great in the Kingdom of Heaven.
Matthew 5:19

Not everyone who calls out to me, "Lord! Lord!" will enter the Kingdom of Heaven. Only those who actually do the will of my Father in heaven will enter.
Matthew 7:21

Dear friends, you always followed my instructions when I was with you. And now that I am away, it is even more important. Work hard to show the results of your salvation, obeying God with deep reverence and fear. For God is working in you, giving you the desire and the power to do what pleases him.
Philippians 2:12-13

When you fall short of God's commands . . .

Keep putting into practice all you learned and received from me—everything you heard from me and saw me doing. Then the God of peace will be with you.
Philippians 4:9

When you want to be more like Jesus . . .

Jesus said to the people who believed in him, "You are truly my disciples if you remain faithful to my teachings."
John 8:31

OPPORTUNITIES

When it seems a door has closed . . .

I can do everything through Christ, who gives me strength.
Philippians 4:13

I know all the things you do, and I have opened a door for you that no one can close. You have little strength, yet you obeyed my word and did not deny me.
Revelation 3:8

When you seek God's timing . . .

God is the one who provides seed for the farmer and then bread to eat. In the same way, he will provide and increase your resources and then produce a great harvest of generosity in you.
2 Corinthians 9:10

When you think there isn't a chance . . .

What is impossible for people is possible with God.
Luke 18:27

When you want to make the most of your opportunities . . .

Well done, my good and faithful servant. You have been faithful in handling this small amount, so now I will give you many more responsibilities.
Matthew 25:21

PAST

When you have regrets about your past . . .

Oh, what joy for those whose disobedience is forgiven, whose sins are put out of sight. Yes, what joy for those whose record the LORD has cleared of sin.

Romans 4:7-8

This means that anyone who belongs to Christ has become a new person. The old life is gone; a new life has begun!

2 Corinthians 5:17

I will forgive their wickedness, and I will never again remember their sins.

Hebrews 8:12

Give all your worries and cares to God, for he cares about you.

1 Peter 5:7

When you give your past, present, and future to God . . .

We have a priceless inheritance—an inheritance that is kept in heaven for you, pure and undefiled, beyond the reach of change and decay. And through your faith, God is protecting you by his power until you receive this salvation, which is ready to be revealed on the last day for all to see.

1 Peter 1:4-5

"I am the Alpha and the Omega—the beginning and the end," says the Lord God. "I am the one who is, who always was, and who is still to come—the Almighty One."

Revelation 1:8

PATIENCE

When it's hard to be patient with someone . . .

May God, who gives this patience and encouragement, help you live in complete harmony with each other, as is fitting for followers of Christ Jesus.

Romans 15:5

When you wait for God's timing . . .

The LORD is good to those who depend on him, to those who search for him. So it is good to wait quietly for salvation from the LORD.

Lamentations 3:25-26

When you get restless . . .

I waited patiently for the LORD to help me, and he turned to me and heard my cry.

Psalm 40:1

When you think you can't take it anymore . . .

Those who trust in the LORD will find new strength. They will soar high on wings like eagles. They will run and not grow weary. They will walk and not faint.

Isaiah 40:31

PERSEVERANCE

When you feel like giving up . . .

Keep on asking, and you will receive what you ask for. Keep on seeking, and you will find. Keep on knocking, and the door will be opened to you.

Luke 11:9

When you need a goal to keep you going . . .

If we are faithful to the end, trusting God just as firmly as when we first believed, we will share in all that belongs to Christ.

Hebrews 3:14

POWER OF GOD

When it seems the world has forgotten who God is and what he can do . . .

Be still, and know that I am God! I will be honored by every nation. I will be honored throughout the world.

Psalm 46:10

You are the God of great wonders! You demonstrate your awesome power among the nations.

Psalm 77:14

When you feel powerless . . .

With God's help we will do mighty things, for he will trample down our foes.

Psalm 60:12

He gives power to the weak and strength to the powerless.

Isaiah 40:29

When you need to be reminded just how powerful your God is . . .

Mightier than the violent raging of the seas, mightier than the breakers on the shore—the LORD above is mightier than these!

Psalm 93:4

This is what the LORD says—your Redeemer and Creator:
"I am the LORD, who made all things. I alone stretched out
the heavens. Who was with me when I made the earth?"
Isaiah 44:24

When you need the power of God to make a lasting change . . .

I am not ashamed of this Good News about Christ. It is the
power of God at work, saving everyone who believes—the
Jew first and also the Gentile.
Romans 1:16

God is working in you, giving you the desire and the power
to do what pleases him.
Philippians 2:13

PRAYER

When you need to sense the presence of God . . .

The LORD is close to all who call on him, yes, to all who call
on him in truth.
Psalm 145:18

When you pray, I will listen. If you look for me wholeheartedly, you will find me.
Jeremiah 29:12-13

He has reconciled you to himself through the death of Christ
in his physical body. As a result, he has brought you into his
own presence, and you are holy and blameless as you stand
before him without a single fault.
Colossians 1:22

When you're concerned your worries are too trivial to bring to God . . .

Don't worry about anything; instead, pray about everything. Tell God what you need, and thank him for all he has done. Then you will experience God's peace, which exceeds anything we can understand. His peace will guard your hearts and minds as you live in Christ Jesus.

Philippians 4:6-7

When you want to strengthen your communication with God . . .

Confess your sins to each other and pray for each other so that you may be healed. The earnest prayer of a righteous person has great power and produces wonderful results.

James 5:16

Treat your wife with understanding as you live together. . . . Treat her as you should so your prayers will not be hindered.

1 Peter 3:7

The eyes of the Lord watch over those who do right, and his ears are open to their prayers.

1 Peter 3:12

PRIDE

When you are so sure that your way is the only way . . .

What sorrow for those who are wise in their own eyes and think themselves so clever.

Isaiah 5:21

When you wonder why pride is such a big deal . . .

When he had become powerful, he also became proud, which led to his downfall.
2 Chronicles 26:16

Pride goes before destruction, and haughtiness before a fall.
Proverbs 16:18

Those who exalt themselves will be humbled, and those who humble themselves will be exalted.
Matthew 23:12

When you have a need to feel important . . .

Anyone who becomes as humble as this little child is the greatest in the Kingdom of Heaven.
Matthew 18:4

As the Scriptures say, "If you want to boast, boast only about the Lord." When people commend themselves, it doesn't count for much. The important thing is for the Lord to commend them.
2 Corinthians 10:17-18

PROBLEMS

When it feels like you're stumbling around in the dark . . .

You light a lamp for me. The Lord, my God, lights up my darkness.
Psalm 18:28

Let those who are wise understand these things. Let those with discernment listen carefully. The paths of the Lord are true and right, and righteous people live by walking in them. But in those paths sinners stumble and fall.
Hosea 14:9

The temptations in your life are no different from what others experience. And God is faithful. He will not allow the temptation to be more than you can stand. When you are tempted, he will show you a way out so that you can endure.

1 Corinthians 10:13

When it seems like God isn't going to save you from your problems . . .

We can rejoice, too, when we run into problems and trials, for we know that they help us develop endurance. And endurance develops strength of character, and character strengthens our confident hope of salvation. And this hope will not lead to disappointment. For we know how dearly God loves us, because he has given us the Holy Spirit to fill our hearts with his love.

Romans 5:3-5

When you see trouble all around you . . .

You are my hiding place; you protect me from trouble. You surround me with songs of victory.

Psalm 32:7

When you panic . . .

God is our refuge and strength, always ready to help in times of trouble. So we will not fear when earthquakes come and the mountains crumble into the sea.

Psalm 46:1-2

When you wonder what God can do . . .

He gives justice to the oppressed and food to the hungry. The LORD frees the prisoners. The LORD opens the eyes of the blind. The LORD lifts up those who are weighed down. The LORD loves the godly.

Psalm 146:7-8

Trust in the LORD with all your heart; do not depend on your own understanding. Seek his will in all you do, and he will show you which path to take.

Proverbs 3:5-6

When you wish someone else could carry your problems . . .

He was pierced for our rebellion, crushed for our sins. He was beaten so we could be whole. He was whipped so we could be healed. All of us, like sheep, have strayed away. We have left God's paths to follow our own. Yet the LORD laid on him the sins of us all.

Isaiah 53:5-6

PRODUCTIVITY

When you want to produce good results . . .

Remain in me, and I will remain in you. For a branch cannot produce fruit if it is severed from the vine, and you cannot be fruitful unless you remain in me. Yes, I am the vine; you are the branches. Those who remain in me, and I in them, will produce much fruit. For apart from me you can do nothing.

John 15:4-5

You died to the power of the law when you died with Christ. And now you are united with the one who was raised from the dead. As a result, we can produce a harvest of good deeds for God.

Romans 7:4

PURPOSE

When you wonder what life is all about . . .

You made all the delicate, inner parts of my body and knit me together in my mother's womb. . . . You saw me before I was born. Every day of my life was recorded in your book. Every moment was laid out before a single day had passed. How precious are your thoughts about me, O God. They cannot be numbered!

Psalm 139:13, 16-17

We don't live for ourselves or die for ourselves. If we live, it's to honor the Lord. And if we die, it's to honor the Lord. So whether we live or die, we belong to the Lord. . . . Yes, each of us will give a personal account to God.

Romans 14:7-8, 12

When you wonder how God can use you . . .

I cry out to God Most High, to God who will fulfill his purpose for me.

Psalm 57:2

My dear brothers and sisters, be strong and immovable. Always work enthusiastically for the Lord, for you know that nothing you do for the Lord is ever useless.

1 Corinthians 15:58

When you want to be ready to carry out God's plans for your life . . .

If you try to hang on to your life, you will lose it. But if you give up your life for my sake, you will save it.

Matthew 16:25

If you keep yourself pure, you will be a special utensil for honorable use. Your life will be clean, and you will be ready for the Master to use you for every good work.

2 Timothy 2:21

RECONCILIATION

When you want to know the way back to a relationship with God . . .

This includes you who were once far away from God. You were his enemies, separated from him by your evil thoughts and actions. Yet now he has reconciled you to himself through the death of Christ in his physical body. As a result, he has brought you into his own presence, and you are holy and blameless as you stand before him without a single fault.

Colossians 1:21-22

There is only one God and one Mediator who can reconcile God and humanity—the man Christ Jesus. He gave his life to purchase freedom for everyone.

1 Timothy 2:5-6

When you want to know the way back to a relationship with someone else . . .

When you are praying, first forgive anyone you are holding a grudge against, so that your Father in heaven will forgive your sins, too.

Mark 11:25

May God, who gives this patience and encouragement, help
you live in complete harmony with each other, as is fitting for
followers of Christ Jesus. Then all of you can join together
with one voice, giving praise and glory to God, the Father
of our Lord Jesus Christ. Therefore, accept each other just
as Christ has accepted you so that God will be given glory.
Romans 15:5-7

REJECTION

**When your circumstances make you feel that God has
rejected you . . .**

The sacrifice you desire is a broken spirit. You will not reject
a broken and repentant heart, O God.
Psalm 51:17

The LORD will not reject his people; he will not abandon his
special possession.
Psalm 94:14

Those the Father has given me will come to me, and I will
never reject them.
John 6:37

When you fear rejection . . .

The needy will not be ignored forever; the hopes of the poor
will not always be crushed.
Psalm 9:18

I am leaving you with a gift—peace of mind and heart. And
the peace I give is a gift the world cannot give. So don't be
troubled or afraid.
John 14:27

We are hunted down, but never abandoned by God. We get knocked down, but we are not destroyed.

2 Corinthians 4:9

When you are tempted to reject the Lord . . .

Solomon, my son, learn to know the God of your ancestors intimately. Worship and serve him with your whole heart and a willing mind. For the LORD sees every heart and knows every plan and thought. If you seek him, you will find him. But if you forsake him, he will reject you forever.

1 Chronicles 28:9

RESPECT

When you show reverence for God . . .

The LORD watches over those who fear him, those who rely on his unfailing love.

Psalm 33:18

When you want to earn the respect of others . . .

Those who are righteous will be long remembered. . . .
Their good deeds will be remembered forever. They will have influence and honor.

Psalm 112:6, 9

If your enemies are hungry, feed them. If they are thirsty, give them something to drink. In doing this, you will heap burning coals of shame on their heads.

Romans 12:20

When others don't respect your beliefs . . .

You must worship Christ as Lord of your life. And if someone asks about your Christian hope, always be ready to explain it. But do this in a gentle and respectful way. Keep your conscience clear. Then if people speak against you, they will be ashamed when they see what a good life you live because you belong to Christ.

1 Peter 3:15-16

RESPONSIBILITY

When you're faithful with what you've been given . . .

To those who use well what they are given, even more will be given, and they will have an abundance. But from those who do nothing, even what little they have will be taken away.

Matthew 25:29

If you are faithful in little things, you will be faithful in large ones. But if you are dishonest in little things, you won't be honest with greater responsibilities.

Luke 16:10

When you're tempted to make excuses . . .

Don't excuse yourself by saying, "Look, we didn't know." For God understands all hearts, and he sees you. He who guards your soul knows you knew. He will repay all people as their actions deserve.

Proverbs 24:12

When you're thinking about your responsibility to God . . .

Don't be misled—you cannot mock the justice of God. You will always harvest what you plant.

Galatians 6:7

No discipline is enjoyable while it is happening—it's painful! But afterward there will be a peaceful harvest of right living for those who are trained in this way.

Hebrews 12:11

SALVATION

When you need to be sure about your salvation . . .

[Jesus says,] "I tell you the truth, those who listen to my message and believe in God who sent me have eternal life. They will never be condemned for their sins, but they have already passed from death into life."

John 5:24

If you confess with your mouth that Jesus is Lord and believe in your heart that God raised him from the dead, you will be saved.

Romans 10:9

Everyone who calls on the name of the LORD will be saved.

Romans 10:13

When you need to know the reason for your salvation . . .

God loved the world so much that he gave his one and only Son, so that everyone who believes in him will not perish but have eternal life.

John 3:16

We know that our old sinful selves were crucified with Christ so that sin might lose its power in our lives. We are no longer slaves to sin. For when we died with Christ we were set free from the power of sin.

Romans 6:6-7

You were dead because of your sins and because your sinful nature was not yet cut away. Then God made you alive with Christ, for he forgave all our sins.

Colossians 2:13

When you're wondering what happens to you inside when you're saved . . .

Through [Christ] God reconciled everything to himself. He made peace with everything in heaven and on earth by means of Christ's blood on the cross. This includes you who were once far away from God. You were his enemies, separated from him by your evil thoughts and actions. Yet now he has reconciled you to himself through the death of Christ in his physical body. As a result, he has brought you into his own presence, and you are holy and blameless as you stand before him without a single fault.

Colossians 1:20-22

SELF-CONTROL

When you want to see lasting changes . . .

All athletes are disciplined in their training. They do it to win a prize that will fade away, but we do it for an eternal prize.

1 Corinthians 9:25

When your thoughts are hard to control . . .

Those who are dominated by the sinful nature think about sinful things, but those who are controlled by the Holy Spirit think about things that please the Spirit. So letting your sinful nature control your mind leads to death. But letting the Spirit control your mind leads to life and peace.

Romans 8:5-6

Fix your thoughts on what is true, and honorable, and right, and pure, and lovely, and admirable. Think about things that are excellent and worthy of praise.

Philippians 4:8

SERVICE

When it's hard to give up more of your time or resources . . .

If you try to hang on to your life, you will lose it. But if you give up your life for my sake, you will save it.

Matthew 16:25

God has given each of you a gift from his great variety of spiritual gifts. Use them well to serve one another. . . . Do you have the gift of helping others? Do it with all the strength and energy that God supplies.

1 Peter 4:10-11

When you want to be a servant leader . . .

You know that the rulers in this world lord it over their people, and officials flaunt their authority over those under them. But among you it will be different. Whoever wants to be a leader among you must be your servant, and whoever wants to be first among you must be the slave of everyone else. For even the Son of Man came not to be served but to serve others and to give his life as a ransom for many.

Mark 10:42-45

When God is prompting you to help others . . .

God . . . will not forget how hard you have worked for him and how you have shown your love to him by caring for other believers, as you still do. Our great desire is that you will keep on loving others as long as life lasts, in order to make certain that what you hope for will come true. Then you will not become spiritually dull and indifferent. Instead, you will follow the example of those who are going to inherit God's promises because of their faith and endurance.

Hebrews 6:10-12

If someone has enough money to live well and sees a brother or sister in need but shows no compassion—how can God's love be in that person? Dear children, let's not merely say that we love each other; let us show the truth by our actions. Our actions will show that we belong to the truth, so we will be confident when we stand before God.

1 John 3:17-19

SIN

When you start thinking sin isn't such a big deal . . .

It's your sins that have cut you off from God. Because of your sins, he has turned away and will not listen anymore.

Isaiah 59:2

For the wages of sin is death, but the free gift of God is eternal life through Christ Jesus our Lord.

Romans 6:23

When you need to be forgiven . . .

Brothers, listen! We are here to proclaim that through this man Jesus there is forgiveness for your sins.

Acts 13:38

When the desire to do wrong seems to overpower your desire to do right . . .

We know that our old sinful selves were crucified with Christ so that sin might lose its power in our lives. We are no longer slaves to sin. For when we died with Christ we were set free from the power of sin.

Romans 6:6-7

When the world seems hopelessly cursed . . .

The next day John saw Jesus coming toward him and said, "Look! The Lamb of God who takes away the sin of the world!"

John 1:29

SPIRITUAL DRYNESS

When you feel spiritually dull . . .

Feed the hungry, and help those in trouble. Then your light will shine out from the darkness, and the darkness around you will be as bright as noon. The LORD will guide you continually, giving you water when you are dry and restoring your strength. You will be like a well-watered garden, like an ever-flowing spring.

Isaiah 58:10-11

Our great desire is that you will keep on loving others as long as life lasts, in order to make certain that what you hope for will come true. Then you will not become spiritually dull and indifferent. Instead, you will follow the example of those who are going to inherit God's promises because of their faith and endurance.

Hebrews 6:11-12

When troubles rob you of your joy . . .

Those who look to him for help will be radiant with joy; no shadow of shame will darken their faces. . . . Taste and see that the LORD is good. Oh, the joys of those who take refuge in him!

Psalm 34:5, 8

My heart is breaking as I remember how it used to be. . . . Why am I discouraged? Why is my heart so sad? I will put my hope in God! I will praise him again—my Savior and my God!

Psalm 42:4-6

SPIRITUAL WARFARE

When you wonder if the enemy is real . . .

A final word: Be strong in the Lord and in his mighty power. Put on all of God's armor so that you will be able to stand firm against all strategies of the devil. For we are not fighting against flesh-and-blood enemies, but against evil rulers and authorities of the unseen world, against mighty powers in this dark world, and against evil spirits in the heavenly places.

Ephesians 6:10-12

When the evil around you seems powerful . . .

Humble yourselves before God. Resist the devil, and he will flee from you.

James 4:7

The devil, who had deceived them, was thrown into the fiery lake of burning sulfur, joining the beast and the false prophet. There they will be tormented day and night forever and ever.

Revelation 20:10

When you want to be on God's side . . .

Endure suffering along with me, as a good soldier of Christ Jesus. . . . I am willing to endure anything if it will bring salvation and eternal glory in Christ Jesus to those God has chosen. This is a trustworthy saying: If we die with him, we will also live with him. If we endure hardship, we will reign with him. If we deny him, he will deny us. If we are unfaithful, he remains faithful, for he cannot deny who he is.

2 Timothy 2:3, 10-13

Don't you realize that friendship with the world makes you an enemy of God? I say it again: If you want to be a friend of the world, you make yourself an enemy of God. What do you think the Scriptures mean when they say that the spirit God has placed within us is filled with envy? But he gives us even more grace to stand against such evil desires.

James 4:4-6

STRENGTH

When you lack the strength to keep going . . .

It is not by force nor by strength, but by my Spirit, says the
LORD of Heaven's Armies.

Zechariah 4:6

I pray that from his glorious, unlimited resources he will
empower you with inner strength through his Spirit. . . .
Then you will be made complete with all the fullness of life
and power that comes from God.

Ephesians 3:16, 19

When you need a strong foundation . . .

I love you, LORD; you are my strength. The LORD is my rock,
my fortress, and my savior; my God is my rock, in whom I
find protection. He is my shield, the power that saves me,
and my place of safety. . . . In your strength I can crush an
army; with my God I can scale any wall.

Psalm 18:1-2, 29

Anyone who listens to my teaching and follows it is wise,
like a person who builds a house on solid rock. Though the
rain comes in torrents and the floodwaters rise and the winds
beat against that house, it won't collapse because it is built on
bedrock.

Matthew 7:24-25

**When you want to experience more of God's strength
in your life . . .**

I also pray that you will understand the incredible greatness of
God's power for us who believe him. This is the same mighty
power that raised Christ from the dead and seated him in the
place of honor at God's right hand in the heavenly realms.

Ephesians 1:19-20

God has not given us a spirit of fear and timidity, but of power, love, and self-discipline.

2 Timothy 1:7

When you need supernatural strength . . .

Who is God except the LORD? Who but our God is a solid rock? God arms me with strength, and he makes my way perfect.

Psalm 18:31-32

✎ SUCCESS

When you're waiting for God to open doors . . .

We know that God causes everything to work together for the good of those who love God and are called according to his purpose for them.

Romans 8:28

We are God's masterpiece. He has created us anew in Christ Jesus, so we can do the good things he planned for us long ago.

Ephesians 2:10

This is the message from the one who is holy and true, the one who has the key of David. What he opens, no one can close; and what he closes, no one can open.

Revelation 3:7

When you want to be successful in God's eyes . . .

Study this Book of Instruction continually. Meditate on it day and night so you will be sure to obey everything written in it. Only then will you prosper and succeed in all you do.

Joshua 1:8

How great is the goodness you have stored up for those who fear you. You lavish it on those who come to you for protection, blessing them before the watching world.

Psalm 31:19

Blessed are those who trust in the LORD and have made the LORD their hope and confidence.

Jeremiah 17:7

SUFFERING

When you've hit rock bottom . . .

He lifted me out of the pit of despair, out of the mud and the mire. He set my feet on solid ground and steadied me as I walked along.

Psalm 40:2

When you wonder if God understands what you're going through . . .

Sing for joy, O heavens! Rejoice, O earth! Burst into song, O mountains! For the LORD has comforted his people and will have compassion on them in their suffering.

Isaiah 49:13

The Holy Spirit helps us in our weakness. For example, we don't know what God wants us to pray for. But the Holy Spirit prays for us with groanings that cannot be expressed in words. And the Father who knows all hearts knows what the Spirit is saying, for the Spirit pleads for us believers in harmony with God's own will.

Romans 8:26-27

When you need to be comforted . . .

All praise to God, the Father of our Lord Jesus Christ.
God is our merciful Father and the source of all comfort.
He comforts us in all our troubles so that we can comfort
others. When they are troubled, we will be able to give them
the same comfort God has given us. For the more we suffer
for Christ, the more God will shower us with his comfort
through Christ.
  2 Corinthians 1:3-5

When you need hope . . .

In his kindness God called you to share in his eternal glory by
means of Christ Jesus. So after you have suffered a little while,
he will restore, support, and strengthen you, and he will place
you on a firm foundation.
  1 Peter 5:10

TALK

When you want your words to help, not hurt . . .

May the words of my mouth and the meditation of my heart
be pleasing to you, O LORD, my rock and my redeemer.
  Psalm 19:14

Timely advice is lovely, like golden apples in a silver basket.
  Proverbs 25:11

Don't use foul or abusive language. Let everything you
say be good and helpful, so that your words will be an
encouragement to those who hear them.
  Ephesians 4:29

When you wonder why you say certain things . . .

Whatever is in your heart determines what you say. A good person produces good things from the treasury of a good heart, and an evil person produces evil things from the treasury of an evil heart. And I tell you this, you must give an account on judgment day for every idle word you speak. The words you say will either acquit you or condemn you.

Matthew 12:34-37

When your tongue gets you into trouble . . .

Does anyone want to live a life that is long and prosperous? Then keep your tongue from speaking evil and your lips from telling lies!

Psalm 34:12-13

You must all be quick to listen, slow to speak, and slow to get angry.

James 1:19

When people accuse you for your faith . . .

He will send help from heaven to rescue me, disgracing those who hound me. . . . My God will send forth his unfailing love and faithfulness.

Psalm 57:3

The apostles left the high council rejoicing that God had counted them worthy to suffer disgrace for the name of Jesus.

Acts 5:41

Be happy when you are insulted for being a Christian, for then the glorious Spirit of God rests upon you.

1 Peter 4:14

TEMPTATION

When you're tempted to look where you shouldn't . . .

Do not let sin control the way you live; do not give in to sinful desires. Do not let any part of your body become an instrument of evil to serve sin. Instead, give yourselves completely to God, for you were dead, but now you have new life. So use your whole body as an instrument to do what is right for the glory of God. Sin is no longer your master, for you no longer live under the requirements of the law. Instead, you live under the freedom of God's grace.

Romans 6:12-14

You belong to God, my dear children. You have already won a victory over those people, because the Spirit who lives in you is greater than the spirit who lives in the world.

1 John 4:4

When you're trusting in your own strength to stand firm . . .

If you think you are standing strong, be careful not to fall. The temptations in your life are no different from what others experience. And God is faithful. He will not allow the temptation to be more than you can stand. When you are tempted, he will show you a way out so that you can endure.

1 Corinthians 10:12-13

He gives us even more grace to stand against such evil desires. As the Scriptures say, "God opposes the proud but favors the humble." So humble yourselves before God. Resist the devil, and he will flee from you.

James 4:6-7

When you call on the Lord for help . . .

Do what is good and run from evil so that you may live! Then
the LORD God of Heaven's Armies will be your helper, just as
you have claimed.
   Amos 5:14

THOUGHTS

When you need help controlling your thoughts . . .

Those who are dominated by the sinful nature think about
sinful things, but those who are controlled by the Holy Spirit
think about things that please the Spirit. So letting your sinful
nature control your mind leads to death. But letting the Spirit
control your mind leads to life and peace.
   Romans 8:5-6

When you wonder how to renew your thought life . . .

Now, dear brothers and sisters, one final thing. Fix your
thoughts on what is true, and honorable, and right, and
pure, and lovely, and admirable. Think about things that are
excellent and worthy of praise. Keep putting into practice all
you learned and received from me—everything you heard
from me and saw me doing. Then the God of peace will be
with you.
   Philippians 4:8-9

When anxiety plagues your thoughts . . .

You will keep in perfect peace all who trust in you, all whose
thoughts are fixed on you!
   Isaiah 26:3

Don't worry about anything; instead, pray about everything.
Tell God what you need, and thank him for all he has done.
  Philippians 4:6

When you wonder how God thinks . . .

The LORD said to Samuel, "Don't judge by his appearance or
height, for I have rejected him. The LORD doesn't see things
the way you see them. People judge by outward appearance,
but the LORD looks at the heart."
  1 Samuel 16:7

TIMING OF GOD

When you don't understand God's timing . . .

God's way is perfect.
  Psalm 18:30

You must not forget this one thing, dear friends: A day is like a
thousand years to the Lord, and a thousand years is like a day.
  2 Peter 3:8

When every day is seen as an opportunity from the Lord . . .

Teach us to realize the brevity of life, so that we may grow
in wisdom.
  Psalm 90:12

When you wonder why Jesus hasn't come back yet . . .

The Lord isn't really being slow about his promise, as some
people think. No, he is being patient for your sake. He does not
want anyone to be destroyed, but wants everyone to repent.
  2 Peter 3:9

TRUTH

When you want to know the truth . . .

All Scripture is inspired by God and is useful to teach us what is true and to make us realize what is wrong in our lives. It corrects us when we are wrong and teaches us to do what is right.

    2 Timothy 3:16

When you wonder why the truth matters . . .

This truth gives them confidence that they have eternal life, which God—who does not lie—promised them before the world began.

    Titus 1:2

When you've been living a lie . . .

Truthful words stand the test of time, but lies are soon exposed.

    Proverbs 12:19

Don't lie to each other, for you have stripped off your old sinful nature and all its wicked deeds. Put on your new nature, and be renewed as you learn to know your Creator and become like him.

    Colossians 3:9-10

Keep a close watch on how you live and on your teaching. Stay true to what is right for the sake of your own salvation and the salvation of those who hear you.

    1 Timothy 4:16

When you wonder if Jesus is the only true way to heaven . . .

Jesus told him, "I am the way, the truth, and the life. No one can come to the Father except through me."

    John 14:6

VICTORY

When you feel defeated . . .

You have rescued me from my troubles and helped me
to triumph over my enemies.

Psalm 54:7

Can anything ever separate us from Christ's love? Does it
mean he no longer loves us if we have trouble or calamity,
or are persecuted, or hungry, or destitute, or in danger, or
threatened with death? (As the Scriptures say, "For your sake
we are killed every day; we are being slaughtered like sheep.")
No, despite all these things, overwhelming victory is ours
through Christ, who loved us.

Romans 8:35-37

When you wonder if God will help you overcome your problems . . .

Don't be afraid, for I am with you. Don't be discouraged, for
I am your God. I will strengthen you and help you. I will
hold you up with my victorious right hand.

Isaiah 41:10

Here on earth you will have many trials and sorrows. But take
heart, because I have overcome the world.

John 16:33

When you need to be reminded of Jesus' ultimate triumph . . .

All who are victorious will be clothed in white. I will never
erase their names from the Book of Life, but I will announce
before my Father and his angels that they are mine.

Revelation 3:5

VIOLENCE

When the violence of the world is overwhelming . . .

Violence will disappear from your land; the desolation and destruction of war will end. Salvation will surround you like city walls, and praise will be on the lips of all who enter there. . . . At the right time, I, the LORD, will make it happen.

Isaiah 60:18, 22

WILL OF GOD

When you are trying to find God's will . . .

The LORD has told you what is good, and this is what he requires of you: to do what is right, to love mercy, and to walk humbly with your God.

Micah 6:8

Dear brothers and sisters, I plead with you to give your bodies to God because of all he has done for you. Let them be a living and holy sacrifice—the kind he will find acceptable. This is truly the way to worship him. Don't copy the behavior and customs of this world, but let God transform you into a new person by changing the way you think. Then you will learn to know God's will for you, which is good and pleasing and perfect.

Romans 12:1-2

When you wish you could know God's plans for your future . . .

"For I know the plans I have for you," says the LORD. "They are plans for good and not for disaster, to give you a future and a hope."

Jeremiah 29:11

When you obey what God commands . . .

If you look carefully into the perfect law that sets you free, and if you do what it says and don't forget what you heard, then God will bless you for doing it.

James 1:25

We are confident that he hears us whenever we ask for anything that pleases him.

1 John 5:14

WITNESSING

When you need a reason to speak out . . .

I tell you the truth, everyone who acknowledges me publicly here on earth, the Son of Man will also acknowledge in the presence of God's angels. But anyone who denies me here on earth will be denied before God's angels.

Luke 12:8-9

Anyone who wants to be my disciple must follow me, because my servants must be where I am. And the Father will honor anyone who serves me.

John 12:26

When you feel awkward talking about Jesus . . .

You will receive power when the Holy Spirit comes upon you. And you will be my witnesses, telling people about me everywhere—in Jerusalem, throughout Judea, in Samaria, and to the ends of the earth.

Acts 1:8

How beautiful are the feet of messengers who bring good news!

Romans 10:15

When you're afraid of how others will respond . . .

I am not ashamed of this Good News about Christ. It is the power of God at work, saving everyone who believes.
  Romans 1:16

WIVES

When you don't understand her . . .

You husbands must give honor to your wives. Treat your wife with understanding as you live together. She may be weaker than you are, but she is your equal partner in God's gift of new life. Treat her as you should so your prayers will not be hindered.
  1 Peter 3:7

When you wonder if you'd be better off alone . . .

Two people are better off than one, for they can help each other succeed. If one person falls, the other can reach out and help. But someone who falls alone is in real trouble. Likewise, two people lying close together can keep each other warm. But how can one be warm alone? A person standing alone can be attacked and defeated, but two can stand back-to-back and conquer.
  Ecclesiastes 4:9-12

When you disagree with her . . .

Since God chose you to be the holy people he loves, you must clothe yourselves with tenderhearted mercy, kindness, humility, gentleness, and patience. Make allowance for each other's faults, and forgive anyone who offends you. Remember, the Lord forgave you, so you must forgive others.
  Colossians 3:12-13

When you want your love to last . . .

Three things will last forever—faith, hope, and love—and the greatest of these is love.

1 Corinthians 13:13

Husbands ought to love their wives as they love their own bodies. For a man who loves his wife actually shows love for himself.

Ephesians 5:28

WORK

When you think your efforts go unnoticed at work . . .

Work willingly at whatever you do, as though you were working for the Lord rather than for people. Remember that the Lord will give you an inheritance as your reward, and that the Master you are serving is Christ.

Colossians 3:23-24

When you feel burned out in your job . . .

The LORD is my shepherd; I have all that I need. He lets me rest in green meadows; he leads me beside peaceful streams. He renews my strength. He guides me along right paths, bringing honor to his name.

Psalm 23:1-3

We now have this light shining in our hearts, but we ourselves are like fragile clay jars containing this great treasure. This makes it clear that our great power is from God, not from ourselves.

2 Corinthians 4:7

When you need a better perspective on your work . . .

Let your good deeds shine out for all to see, so that everyone will praise your heavenly Father.

Matthew 5:16

When you are not sure if God is working in you . . .

I am certain that God, who began the good work within you, will continue his work until it is finally finished on the day when Christ Jesus returns.

Philippians 1:6

WORSHIP

When you have much to be thankful for . . .

It is good to give thanks to the LORD, to sing praises to the Most High.

Psalm 92:1

Let all that I am praise the LORD; with my whole heart, I will praise his holy name. Let all that I am praise the LORD; may I never forget the good things he does for me. He forgives all my sins and heals all my diseases. He redeems me from death and crowns me with love and tender mercies. He fills my life with good things.

Psalm 103:1-5

When you need a reason to worship . . .

God elevated him to the place of highest honor and gave him the name above all other names, that at the name of Jesus every knee should bow, in heaven and on earth and under the earth, and every tongue confess that Jesus Christ is Lord, to the glory of God the Father.

Philippians 2:9-11

Great and marvelous are your works, O Lord God, the Almighty. Just and true are your ways, O King of the nations. Who will not fear you, Lord, and glorify your name? For you alone are holy. All nations will come and worship before you, for your righteous deeds have been revealed.

Revelation 15:3-4

WORTH

When you feel too insignificant for God to care about you . . .

What is the price of five sparrows—two copper coins? Yet God does not forget a single one of them. And the very hairs on your head are all numbered. So don't be afraid; you are more valuable to God than a whole flock of sparrows.

Luke 12:6-7

We are God's masterpiece. He has created us anew in Christ Jesus, so we can do the good things he planned for us long ago.

Ephesians 2:10

๏ FAVORITE VERSES ๏

May the Lord Bless You

May the LORD bless you and protect you. May the LORD
smile on you and be gracious to you. May the LORD show
you his favor and give you his peace.
Numbers 6:24-26

God Is Your Strength

Some nations boast of their chariots and horses, but we boast
in the name of the LORD our God.
Psalm 20:7

God Is Merciful

Do not remember the rebellious sins of my youth. Remember
me in the light of your unfailing love, for you are merciful,
O LORD.
Psalm 25:7

You Can Start Anew

Create in me a clean heart, O God. Renew a loyal spirit
within me.
Psalm 51:10

God Cares for You

Give your burdens to the LORD, and he will take care of you.
He will not permit the godly to slip and fall.
Psalm 55:22

God Is in Control

You can make many plans, but the LORD's purpose will prevail.
Proverbs 19:21

Work Well

Whatever you do, do well.
Ecclesiastes 9:10

God Is Able

I am the LORD, the God of all the peoples of the world.
Is anything too hard for me?
Jeremiah 32:27

The Lord's Prayer

Our Father in heaven, may your name be kept holy. May your
Kingdom come soon. May your will be done on earth, as it is
in heaven. Give us today the food we need, and forgive us our
sins, as we have forgiven those who sin against us. And don't
let us yield to temptation, but rescue us from the evil one.
Matthew 6:9-13

Setting Priorities

Seek the Kingdom of God above all else, and live righteously,
and he will give you everything you need.
Matthew 6:33

Persistence Is Rewarded

Keep on asking, and you will receive what you ask for. Keep on seeking, and you will find. Keep on knocking, and the door will be opened to you. For everyone who asks, receives. Everyone who seeks, finds. And to everyone who knocks, the door will be opened.

Matthew 7:7-8

God Offers Rest

Come to me, all of you who are weary and carry heavy burdens, and I will give you rest.

Matthew 11:28

Becoming a Child of God

To all who believed him and accepted him, he gave the right to become children of God.

John 1:12

Suffering Is Temporary

What we suffer now is nothing compared to the glory he will reveal to us later.

Romans 8:18

Our Weakness Displays His Strength

Each time [the Lord] said, "My grace is all you need. My power works best in weakness." So now I am glad to boast about my weaknesses, so that the power of Christ can work through me.

2 Corinthians 12:9

Living for Christ

My old self has been crucified with Christ. It is no longer I who live, but Christ lives in me. So I live in this earthly body by trusting in the Son of God, who loved me and gave himself for me.

Galatians 2:20

Pray Continually

Pray in the Spirit at all times and on every occasion. Stay alert and be persistent in your prayers for all believers everywhere.

Ephesians 6:18

Unconditional Thanks

Be thankful in all circumstances, for this is God's will for you who belong to Christ Jesus.

1 Thessalonians 5:18